# The Sales S

## A Crash Course in

## By Matt Lawrence

Published by *Choppa University Press*

www.Choppamedia.com

Table of Contents

# Introduction

Your competition will tell you that the ability to sell is either innate or absent in any individual; if you have it, you have it; If you don't, you don't. You might think you just don't have it because you haven't had much success selling in the past. You might look at charismatic salespeople, orators, and motivators and wonder how they do what they do.

I can already tell you what the trouble might be: The roadblocks obstructing your way to becoming a formidable salesperson begin in your own psyche. Let's do a word association exercise: When surveyed and asked what words and phrases come to mind at the mere mention of the term, "salesman," participants overwhelmingly returned answers like, "greasy," slick," "pushy," "sleazy," and "dishonest." I'm willing to bet you have some of the same visions in your mind of the classic clichéd used-car salesman in his thick, yellow plaid blazer and 1970's comb-over haircut. Perhaps you think about the number of random phone calls you get every day from people in India, calling from sham numbers with your area code, trying to sell you whatever it is they want to sell you.

The fact is, most people have a negative view of salespeople and sales as a whole. Becoming a telemarketer or an in-store sales representative is often a last resort or fallback for a lot of people when they just can't find a job that fits them. Some turn to multi-level direct selling companies only to try again and again to recruit others to their downline in order to avoid selling overpriced and overhyped products to their own friends and family.

Businesses need salespeople, but many entrepreneurs struggle with capturing and conveying the charm required to make others spend money with them. So they hire a team of salespeople. The business owner, having a negative view of sales in general, will inevitably start off on the wrong foot with feelings of resentment towards his new employees, thus forging a rocky relationship and producing sales associates who just won't care.

These negative associations even creep into the actions of those brave souls who attempt to sell without any sort of plan and without learning the necessary skills and proper attitudes to do so successfully. A fear of annoying people with offers or anxiety about asking for money colors their interactions. These feeble attempts at sales are filled with weak, apologetic language: "Hey, sorry to bother you, would you mind if I took some time to tell you about something you might maybe want to possibly buy?" It's not a leap or a bound to say that these "salespeople" are quick to call it quits when they don't end up accomplishing their goals.

Erasing this destructive mentality is the first step to finding success in learning how to sell. The truth is, sales skills are crucial to multiple areas of life and it's also true that most salespeople don't have bad intentions of misleading or swindling others. Successful salespeople genuinely care about fulfilling the wants and needs of the people they serve. They don't take pride in making people spend money they don't have or buy things they will have no use for. A good salesperson is not simply a powerful persuader but a teacher, one who influences and inspires. A good salesperson is driven and empowered by helping others connect with the right solutions to their problems. Noble salespeople emanate positive vibrations and good feelings of certainty, confidence and security.

If you are a business owner reading this book, you might believe that the major problem with your business is low sales. The solution, of course, being higher sales. The problem with that is you're not good at selling. The solution? Get better at selling.

Maybe you're employed as a sales associate at some company, or maybe it's you who's part of a multi-level direct selling operation. If you're reading this book, you feel that your sales are not where you want them to be. The solution? Again, get better at selling.

You have to sell every day of your life. I'm not just talking about at work or in your business. Yes, you do have to sell to make money, but you also have to "sell" your character, your ideas, your beliefs, and your reasoning. You have to be able to get others to work with you, or to go along with your plans. The skills that make up the art of selling are necessary for getting what you want out of life.

When fully and properly adopted, the wonderfully freeing beliefs and workable systems delineated in this book can transform a person with the entirely wrong mindset and no ability to sell into an awe-inspiring force of nature who can move product and sway opinions with only an iota of effort.

# A Word on Inner Game

There are two major components to selling. These are aspects we can call internalization and externalization. They can also be referred to as inner game and outer game respectively. Game refers to one's level of mastery, ability, or proficiency in his or her skill set. For example, you might hear the expression when men chat amongst each other about how good their "game" is in terms of seducing women. You might hear someone say, "I feel off my game today," when they are having a bad day and just can't seem to get anything right. In sales, game is made up of, first, the mindset, attitudes, beliefs, and state of the salesperson (inner game), and second, the specific techniques and routines that can be expended to achieve desired results (outer game). In sales, a combination of good inner and outer game equals consistent interactions culminating in positive transactions.

While the majority of this book contains a step by step breakdown of the sales procedure and other outer game techniques, it must be noted that without the proper internalizations, the processes, routines and language patterns that comprise the coming chapters are only as powerful as the prospect is suggestible and oblivious. Most intelligent people can see through an actor playing a part they don't believe in. People don't like fakes and us humans have become quite adept at sniffing them out, most of the time. If someone is untrustworthy, the involuntary micro-movements of the face and body often give them away. Slight variations in voice tone and diction can set off conscious or subconscious alarm bells that something is off about this individual. Even posture can betray a person's state of mind; An unconfident, anxious or insincere person will reflexively shrink his spine and cover himself with his arms as protective mechanisms, to take up less space in a situation in which he feels unwelcome. Bad liars and perjurers are known to touch their face or mouth when speaking untruths.

The secret therefore, is that in order for a person to seem trustworthy and as having good intentions, the person must actually be trustworthy and have good intentions! Revolutionary, I know. Try to contain your astonishment at this absolute revelation.

Proper inner game is vital to success in this method. Without the right amalgamation of strong ethics and inner game, you're not fit to sell in the first place.

A good salesperson has to radiate genuine trustworthiness over all other characteristics. A prospect has to trust the salesperson if they are going to buy from them. The prospect must also feel respected, and as such, the salesperson must treat their prospect with esteem and couth. The salesperson must be sincerely excited about the idea of improving their prospect's life with the product or service they are offering. The prospect should catch the contagious certainty of the salesperson, who should emit a warm, wonderful confidence and enthusiasm.

Napoleon Hill wrote, "thoughts are things." The thoughts you carry manifest into actions, and these actions are effects from such mental causations. Every effect is in itself another cause to another effect and so on, forever. You see, the things you think in your mind create ripples that transcend your own mind and affect the real world. Negative thoughts have the potential to cause negative effects. These negative thoughts and limiting beliefs are mental patterns that can only be broken by self discipline and an assumption of personal responsibility; It is your responsibility to use the skills you will learn to improve people's lives. It is your responsibility to spread light and certainty.

Self discipline and responsibility are what mobilizes a person to get out of bed and get to work. Willpower and accountability drive a salesperson to call lead after lead, and endure failure after failure until they achieve their goal.

Having an awareness of responsibility can help a person establish meaningful, worthwhile goals and work towards self-improvement, thus increasing their self esteem and overall sense of worth. A person who feels worthy is more likely to associate with positive-minded, joyful people who are encouraging and motivating, as opposed to people who are negative and unnecessarily critical. It contributes to a positive self image: If a person has discipline and takes pride in how they look and dress, they will present themselves as such and exude an unmatched poise, with or without classic good looks or the hottest fashions.

When first going into a sales interaction it is important to enter in a positive state or condition. The proper state for selling anything is one in which you are: One: Sharp and insightful; two: enthusiastic and passionate; and three: a confident authority in your field. It will take some practice to achieve this state. Some people use meditation, others pump themselves up (or calm themselves down) with music or a workout, or by repeating affirmations. The best salespeople just know that these characteristics are true aspects of their true self, and live their lives as such. When this state is correctly achieved and permanently engrained, superficial outer game techniques become less important. Of course, the structure of a sale is always the same and must be followed, but the actions of a self-assured salesperson who produces good vibrations of certitude can undoubtedly outweigh the power of scripted routines. The majority of outer game techniques are used mainly to control conversations and steer them to an end; before, during, and after the proper state has been conveyed and transferred to the prospect.

Be witty and perceptive; Get the prospect to see you as an intelligent and insightful person and source of wisdom. Communicate a real affinity for the product, service, prospect and interaction. Speak clearly and always wear a smile, even on the phone. Express yourself definitely and boldly, as any authority would. If you want to portray an expert, you must feel like an expert. To feel like an expert, you must become an expert: Learn all there is to know about your field. Learn everything about the product or service you are selling. Learn about the history of the industry, and why your solution is better than all the others, beyond the talking points outlined in your pre-written script.

Anyone who has achieved major success will tell you that conquering this mental state is the key to victory in sales and incidentally many other areas of life. This state shouldn't only be adopted during sales interactions but should be a constant factor in your demeanor and conduct.
Do not neglect your inner game. It's up to you to figure out how you will achieve this essential mental transformation and it's your responsibility to uphold it once it's been attained. You will see the true power of belief when the good vibrations you put out return to you in both material and immaterial ways.

# The Hollywood Method: Explained

In everything there is manifested a measured motion. For every cause, there is an effect. Events happen in sequence. Everything and every action in the physical world is measurable and can be broken down into smaller parts. With an understanding of each part of a thing, it is possible to discern the patterns and nature therein. Mathematics and science provide us with formulas to arrive at conclusions to our many questions. Even recipes call for specific ingredients and prescribe exact instructions. So why then, do people go at anything in life without taking time to dissect the situation and determine the formulas embedded within? When is it ever a good idea to begin an endeavor without a plan? A sale is no different. A sale is an exact process; A sequence of events that begins at an introduction and ends with a transaction. If one can remain in control of the sequence, the path and the outcome will always remain the same.

After studying the many varied approaches of some of the best salespeople in history, as well as experiencing firsthand years of trial and error, I can safely say that I have cracked the code to the sales sequence. I have developed a universal system of selling that works, not only for me, but for every single person I've ever taught it to. Not only that, but this system works in every sales interaction from retail to cold calling, with only minor tweaks and customizations per situation. Even in one's personal life, this system I have developed is a methodical tool that can be applied across the board to persuade and motivate others. This method is the "outer game" of selling.

One stipulation: A person using this system must work through the steps in order, or face a high probability of failure. That's because the steps follow the exact logical and emotional progression of decision-making. Taking the steps out of order will disrupt that process in the prospect and may even upset or insult them. It's like going on a date; If the first thing you say to your blind date when meeting for the first time is, "Hello, how about we go back to my place?" there's a good chance they'll be put off and won't be going back to your place. Likewise, with a sale; if you call up an unsuspecting prospect and start by saying, "hello, would you like to buy something from me?" you'll likely hear a dial tone before you're even able to tell the prospect what it is you're selling.

I call my system of sales, "The Hollywood Method," because it flows much like a movie; It is broken into three acts: The Exposition, the Staging, and the Climax. Each of these acts is again segmented into three parts, the details of which we will cover in subsequent chapters. A brief description of each will be provided here in this chapter as well.

 "The Hollywood Method," puts the salesperson in the role of a performer and the prospect in the role of the audience. In each step, the salesperson performs "routines," or specifically worded phrases that move the interaction forward and keep the salesperson in control. From a foundation of Neuro-Linguistic Programming, routines in this system are based on language patterns that have been proven to encourage compliance. Delivery of the routines is just as important as the words being said. A full sequence of routines, from act one through act three, is called a "set." The end result of performing a good set is an agreement and transaction; monetary or otherwise.

Act one, the Exposition, is where the interaction begins. It is broken into three parts: The Opening, The Hook, and Qualification. The Opening is where the salesperson is introduced and begins to build rapport with the prospect. The Hook is a point early in the interaction where the prospect agrees to talk and becomes intrigued enough to hear what the salesperson has to say. Next, Qualification is the step in which the salesperson asks pertinent questions to uncover the problem the prospect is looking to solve, as well as their wants, their needs and how much they can spend.

Act two is called the Staging. In this stage, the prospect is presented with the idea, product or service. The first step in the Staging is the Presentation. This step is straightforward and involves telling the prospect about the offering in factual terms. The next step is called Logical Reasoning, and in this step, the prospect is presented with rational, analytical arguments as to why they should go along with the sale. This could be in the form of a lucrative price, or confirmation that the features of the product or service align with what the prospect is looking for. The last step in act two is Emotional Reasoning. In this step, the salesperson causes the prospect to conjure up feelings of pain that they will associate with not buying, and then to imagine the pleasure they will derive from going through with it and actually buying.

Act three is the Climax. It begins with a concept I call, "the False Close." In this step, the salesperson asks the prospect to buy or make a decision for the first time in the interaction. This is usually where a prospect begins to think of reasons and excuses as to why they can't or don't want to buy– even though they just spent however long talking to a salesperson. The thought of parting with money can often trigger anxiety and emotional distress and so we come to the next stage, called Overcoming Objections. This is the belly of the beast, or the final climactic battle in a film. In this stage, the salesperson handles all the protests, doubts and concerns that prevent the prospect from making a "yes" decision right then and there. These objections are common, and can often be quashed with pre-written, "canned" routines. Finally, when all logical and emotional arguments against buying are nullified and the prospect can't say no, the salesperson can again employ pre-written, canned routines to close the sale and move along with an agreement and transaction.

I developed this method so I could quickly and easily create sales scripts, on the fly, for the wide variety of products and services that my companies provide. In doing so, I discovered that the system works for much, much more and could be of great significance to many people. This book contains a comprehensive explanation of each aspect of this process and includes a lot of great, effective routines that can be employed every step of the way. Internalizing this easy, step-by-step process will help you to get what you want in business, and in life, with as little resistance as possible.

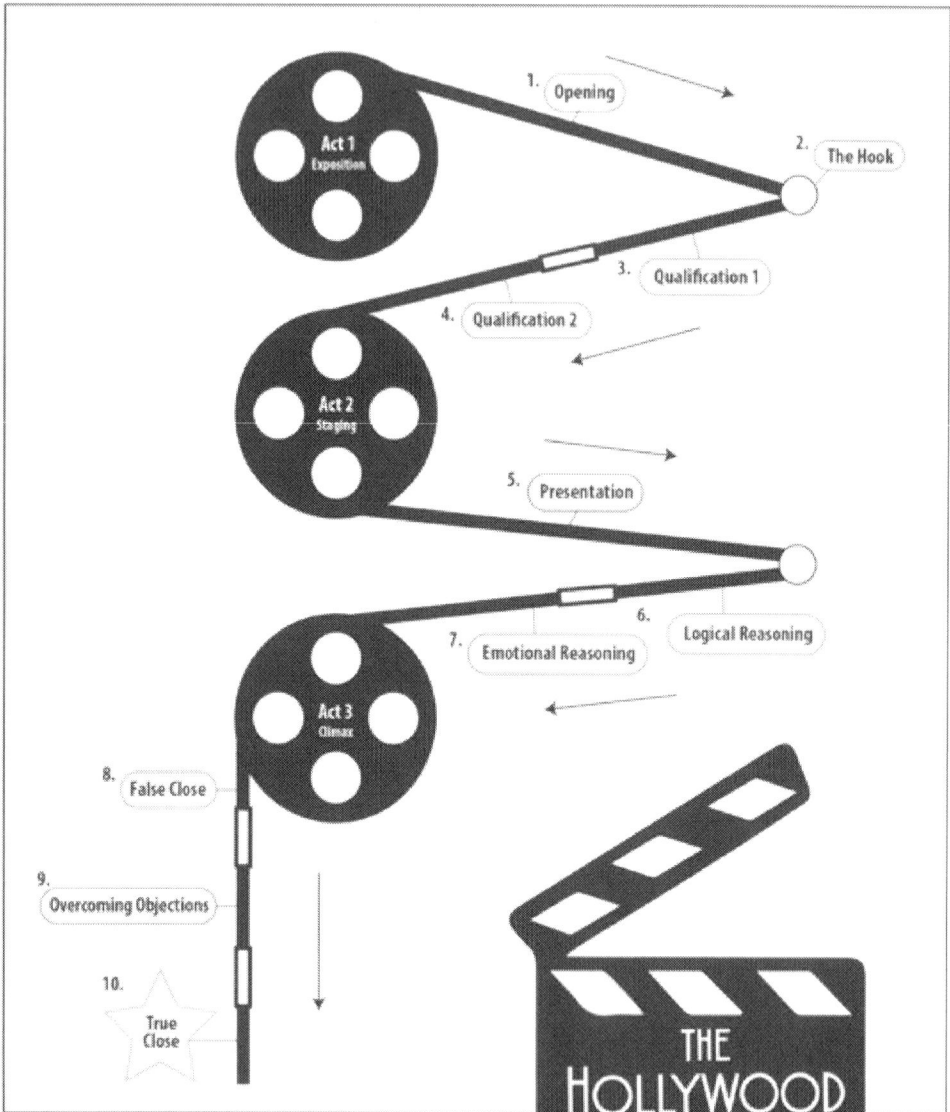

1. Opening
2. The Hook
3. Qualification 1
4. Qualification 2
5. Presentation
6. Logical Reasoning
7. Emotional Reasoning
8. False Close
9. Overcoming Objections
10. True Close

Act 1
Exposition

Act 2
Staging

Act 3
Climax

THE HOLLYWOOD METHOD™

# Act One: The Exposition

## Opening

The only place to begin is the beginning. The beginning of the sales conversation sets the stage for the entire event. How you start a conversation is immensely important and will determine if you even make it to step two. We call this first step in the interaction, "opening." We will use the term in multiple ways, for example, you can "open" a conversation or you an "open" a prospect. You can use "openers," or scripted routines specifically formulated to engage the prospect.

Before explaining in detail about how to properly open, it pays to know who you are supposed to open in the first place. You don't open strangers; you open "leads." Leads come from the efforts put into your company's marketing. Leads, to put it simply, are prospects. Successful marketing should generate specifically targeted prospects who already have an interest in the brand, product, service, idea, or experience you are selling. The marketing efforts put forth by a company should establish lines of communication between the company and its customers. It's up to a salesperson to foster that communication and move it to an end where both parties are satisfied. If you are a sales associate employed at a company, you must use the notes and data provided to you by your marketing department to engage in honest dialogues. It also helps to do your own due diligence on your prospects. If you are a retail sales associate in a store or boutique, the shoppers who enter your store are people who buy items of that brand, or style or price range. They were brought to that particular store by the parent company's marketing efforts. If you are an entrepreneur or business owner in charge of your own marketing, read my book, "Marketing Mantra: A Crash Course in Brand Building." It's a short and to-the-point book that will teach you how to create a focused and coherent marketing plan that will communicate your company's true purpose, and produce targeted leads that will fall in love with your brand.

So can you recognize the opening of a sales conversation? When you walk into a retail store, an associate will ask if there's anything they can help you with or if there's anything you're looking for. They'll make an introduction, tell you their name and say, "if you need anything, just holler." That's an open. When you go to a restaurant, your server starts by telling you their name, asking how you're doing and if you'd like a drink. That's an open. Only after opening can they pitch the night's high-priced specials.

What about a solicitation over the phone? That's an easy one to recognize. Probably because most salespeople get it wrong. Many phone salespeople start off with something like, "I'm so-and-so calling from Company X, we're the best in the industry, yadda yadda yadda." This is a good way to trigger the fight or flight response of the person on the other end. When someone gets a call like this, the first thing they think is, "how can I get rid of this guy?" or they just simply hang up.

Nobody wants to be sold to. Our reflexive instinct is to shut someone down when we know they want to extract money from us. Even if a customer was already in the market to begin with, if a salesperson opens a conversation poorly, it might cause that customer to decide they just want to shop on their own and avoid human contact all together.

Therefore, when opening a sale, the most important thing to remember is to avoid triggering that fight or flight response. You must build instant rapport. Always remain in state and convey that you are enthusiastic, insightful and a confident authority in your industry. In person, a prospect will judge you in less than a second; so make sure your body language is on point: Practice good posture and convey a non-threatening self-assurance and warmth.

The analogy of the salesperson as the performer and the prospect as the audience informs us that the entire experience of any sale, as with any performance, is always for the benefit of the audience, and not the performer. Everything the performer does is for the effect it has on the audience. An audience wants to be entertained, feel a rollercoaster of emotions, and end up satisfied upon the conclusion.

The prospect needs you to answer three important questions in the first fifteen seconds of any sales conversation: "Who are you?" "Why are you calling/talking to me?" And, "What can you do for me?" Volunteer these answers in your opener; don't let the prospect get to a point where he has to ask you for any of the three. The way to do this without triggering that reflexive response is to exercise humility. Don't say something like, "I'm Bob from XYZ, and I'm calling to tell you about this great product we have with all this great stuff that I'd really like you to try!" A prospect doesn't want to hear a list of features right off the bat. They don't care about your company; they don't care about you. Although this example follows all the necessary beats and answers those pertinent questions, none of that statement focuses on the experience of the prospect (the audience) and instead focuses entirely on the salesperson (the performer). Imagine if you met a person at a party and he could do nothing but talk about himself and how great he is. You wouldn't want to talk to that guy very long. That's why it's important to learn about and understand your leads. If you know your prospects, you might have some insight on their "pain," or their "void." These are other words we can use to describe any problems the prospect would benefit from solving. Humbly relaying that you understand their pain and asking if their issue is something you might be able to help with is a much better way to lower those defenses.

Try saying something along the lines of, "Hi [Prospect], this is [Salesperson] from [Company]. I'm calling because we've recently helped a number of companies like yours increase their [important metric] by as much as 40%. I know that there is a lot of pressure on [important metric] these days."

You could also say something like, "Hi [Prospect], this is [Salesperson] from [Company]. We're a local company and we've helped a lot of businesses in the area cut down their [Service] costs and increase their bottom line."

Notice how phrasing your opening in this way communicates that you care. See how much better that is than bragging about the history of your company or features of your product? Using wording like this is a fantastic way to disarm the prospect. Once the prospect's initial apprehension is neutralized, you'll be able to cleanly and seamlessly initiate step two:

**The Hook**

The hook is the second step in the sales procedure. This is the point where the prospect agrees to continue the conversation and hear what the salesperson has to say. The hook is the first agreement in the series of agreements leading up to the final transaction. Hooking the prospect is easy; You can simply say, "May I ask you a few questions to see if there's any chance I might be able to help you?"

You could also say something like, "If you have 60 seconds, I'd like to share an idea with you...got a minute?" Providing such a false time constraint is another method of diffusing the prospect's anxiety. It lets the prospect breathe a sigh of relief that this interaction won't take long. Follow up with, "just a few questions, so I don't waste your time..."

Upon the prospect's agreement with the hook, the interaction will move straight into step three: Qualification.

**Qualification**

Step three of act one is called Qualification, and it is broken into two sub-steps. For ease, we'll call them Q1 and Q2. In sales, qualification is the act of gauging potential prospects to determine if they would be a good fit for your product or service. Asking pertinent questions is how you determine whether or not the prospect is even worth your time. Specifically, in our method, after the prospect has agreed to talk, you must then extract certain pieces of information from them. For one, you have to know what they are lacking in order to know whether or not you can fill their needs. You also have to know their budget, or how much they intend to spend.

## Q1: Gazing Into The Void

Q1 is the first sub-step of the qualification phase. In this step you must figure out the problem the prospect is looking to solve and the gaps in their current situation. We call this discovering the prospect's "void." The void, like the name suggests, is essentially the hole the prospect needs to fill. The void is what causes the prospect pain. Looking into a prospect's void reveals their emotional hot-buttons and triggers that you might be able to use later to motivate them into taking an action. You might already have some sort of an idea of their needs based on the nature of your business or any sort of information that may have been provided to you, but you must follow the procedure and ask the questions that lead to the next step.

What questions do you ask in Q1? You ask open ended questions. While you must adapt your routines to fit your specific industry and prospect, there are some old standards on which you might want to base your lines of questioning: "What challenges are you struggling with?"
"Do you currently have a solution in place?"
"Why hasn't it been addressed before?"
"What does solving this problem mean to you personally?"

"Of all the factors, what's the most important to you in making your business successful?"

"What would you say is your biggest headache when it comes to [Situation]?"

"What happens if you do nothing about [Situation]?"

"What's prevented you from solving [Problem] in the past?"

When you have a solid understanding of the prospect's pain, it can be tempting to jump right into telling them how suitable your solution would be in solving their problems. This, however, would be a misstep. Instead, you need to restrain yourself and move on to Q2.

## Q2: Discovering The Prospect's Investment Potential

In this sub-step, you need to figure out the prospect's "investment potential." How much money can the prospect potentially invest in your product or service? Can they even afford what you're selling?

First things first, before anything else in Q2 you have to determine whether or not the person you're talking to even has the authority to make a purchase or spend money. You don't want to be pitching and presenting to gatekeepers. Ask, "How does your company's decision process work in this area?" or "Who at your company holds the decision-making power when it comes to [Situation]?" If you are indeed speaking to a gatekeeper, they might give you the name of the person you truly seek. From there you can try to reach them directly or attempt to have the gatekeeper establish a line of communication for you.

Most of the time, a person or company's ability to spend is significantly larger than the amount of money they actually intend to spend. Very rarely do you get a client like John Hammond from Jurassic Park, who isn't afraid to "spare no expense." That being said, a common objection people have to buying is price. By properly executing Q2 and learning how much the prospect intends or is able to spend, you can mitigate or even prevent this objection later when it comes to closing.

To ascertain this necessary information, you can use routines like, "Curious, how much do you usually spend on [Service] year to year?" Or, "Do you have a budget allocated for this project?"

Now that you know the prospect has the money and should buy your product, Q2 is complete.

Remember the answers to the qualification questions you asked from both Q1 and Q2. If you are selling on the phone, write them down. If you are selling in person, write them down after the fact. Taking notes at this stage is invaluable because it will help shape the routines you use in Act Two, where you present the features and benefits of your product or service. Keep these notes as a record of your client and you'll be able to sustain a mutually beneficial relationship in which you'll be able to help them again and again.

After the completion of Q2, Act One comes to an end when the salesperson confidently, and with an air of certainty, utters a simple phrase:

"Well let me say this: Based on everything you just told me, it sounds like I actually have something that's a perfect fit for you.

Now, real quick..."

## Act Two: The Staging

Congratulations, you've made it through the most anxiety-inducing part of the Hollywood Method sales formula. You're through with the first act; You've opened a prospect and begun your set. You've gotten key pieces of information that you can now move into play in Act Two.

The second act, like the first, is also made up of three main steps, with the third being broken into two smaller sub-steps. Each part involves speaking about your product or service, but each serves a different function and is executed in its own unique way.

### The Presentation

The first step in Act Two is the presentation. This is the stage in which you present the prospect with the facts about what you're offering. The key in this stage is to explain your proposal in simple terms. You know what your business does, and you know what your product is and you know what you want them to do. There's no need to embellish or use flowery language. In fact, doing so here might even turn the prospect off completely... It's time to talk business. You can start using puffery and captivating their emotions again in a just a few moments, but here, simply communicate exactly what you are offering and what the cost would be.

This stage is complete in just a few sentences. It's quick, it's clean, you're in and you're out. You can now move over the next threshold. In a film, this would be the part in which the hero (the prospect), learns that there is a solution to their problem: The McGuffin; the promised land; the wizard of Oz. Now they know your solution exists, but they're not off to see the wizard just yet. They have only a vague knowledge of your remedy, and to them, it's still off in the distance; no matter how close you may be or how eager you are to close the sale. They have still yet to be convinced to go along with the journey. Now it's time to give them some good reasons. Quickly move on to the next phase, called Logical Reasoning.

## Logical Reasoning

The purpose of this step is to communicate exactly why your solution is the best. Here, you present the prospect with logical, analytical arguments as to why they should go along with your proposal. These factual, positive details are things they have to know. Maybe your product or service has the most competitive price or maybe it makes use of the newest technology. Maybe it's the smallest, most compact, biggest, strongest, toughest, most durable, or most popular. If, by this point, the prospect hasn't already exclaimed, "take my money, please!" they are still on the fence, and truthfully, these logical reasons are probably not going to convince them... But they do serve a purpose: Most decisions are made in the heat of an emotion. People make decisions to increase pleasure and avoid pain. Only after the fact does a person backwards rationalize their impulse decisions with logical arguments. The reasons you describe here are what they'll look back on after purchasing and say, "That's why I bought that," even if you know the *real* reason... Which brings us to the next step; Inciting that real reason; provoking an impulse buy by captivating the prospect's emotions.

## Emotional Reasoning

You might be happy to know that in this stage, you get to use all the fancy, extravagant language you want. This is the part when you really move the prospect emotionally. Imagination is a very powerful thing, and often times even thinking about certain feelings can invoke them. When you've watched films in the past, have you ever cried over a fictional character's misfortune? Have you ever cringed at a fictional character's injury? By leading your prospect's imagination, you can influence their real emotions.

This step, much like the third step in Act One, is made up of two smaller sub-steps which we'll denote in shorthand as E1 and E2. The first is centered around pain and the second, pleasure.

**E1: Pain Re-Stimulation**

Look back to your notes from Q1. What is the prospect's void? What are the gaps in their current situation and what is at stake for them if their problem is not corrected? Remind them. Describe that pain in a dramatic fashion. Remind them of the discomfort that your product or service will alleviate.

Say something like, "You know, I've dealt with a lot of people in your situation, and I understand the position you're in if [Situation] doesn't work out the way you need it to...You're losing money/ You're wasting time/ Your job could be at risk/ Your business could be at risk," and so on.

Make it quick; don't dwell on things that will make the prospect feel pain any longer than they have to. Torture them for too long, and they'll just begin to associate *you* with that pain, and start to believe it's *you* making them feel that way. Stimulating a person's pain for too long will divert their attention from the real source of their anxiety; That which they already told you, and which you are simply repeating back to them.

Therefore, to avoid bumming the prospect out to the point that they no longer want to talk to you, it is now necessary to elicit in them feelings of pleasure.

**E2: Pleasure Visualization**

In E2, you describe the good feelings and gratification the prospect will feel by going along with your plan and buying your product or service. Paint for them a picture of a perfect world where their issues are a thing of the past. Show them a happy future, free from the headaches and apprehension you just took them through in E1. Say something like, "In the long run, if you go through with it and sign up today, you're going to spend a lot less on [Service] going forward," or "If you purchase today, in the long run, you're going increase revenues multiple times over," Tack on something like, "Think of all the time you'll save, think of all those worries you can just do away with for good!"

Let them know buying from you is a smart move that will make them look good; "If you're wearing this, you'll turn a lot of heads, you'll be the focal point of the room," or "Think of how your boss is going to act towards you when you're saving them all this money/ Bringing in all these new customers/ sourcing better supplies..." You get the idea.

The prospect probably likes you enough by now, so solidify this emotional fantasy with a personal endorsement along the lines of: "Believe me, if I'm even half right, and you utilize [Product or Service] for your situation, you'll know that people will take you seriously/ You'll be able to compete with [Competitor]," or whatever else you can think of that's appropriate.

The key here is to make them feel good. They should be laughing and jovial by this point, and hopefully, in an agreeable mood. Most times if you make it to this stage, the prospect's buying temperature is high. Buying temperature refers to how likely a person is to buy something. The higher the buying temperature, the more likely they are to buy.

Next, take advantage of their high buying temperature. Make note of these pleasurable feelings you just talked about and ask your prospect, "Now, does *that* sound like the kind of situation you'd rather be in?" They'll undoubtedly answer "Yes." Who wouldn't say "yes" to experiencing pleasurable feelings? Who wouldn't say "yes" to a life free from certain anxieties?

This isn't the sale though, and just because they answer yes to this question doesn't mean you've closed the deal. However, if you can get them to admit they would be happier with having bought what you're selling, you've almost got them. Moving right along...

# Act Three: The Climax

The third act in a film is usually the most exciting. That's why we call the final act in our sales method, "the climax." This is where things really heat up. This act, like the others, is broken into three simple steps.

Up until this point, you've hopefully been following your script and have not deviated from it. Now though, throughout the most of act three, you get to choose your own adventure, so to speak. In just a moment, you'll get to bust out your own choice of routines and improvise with what the prospect throws at you.

First things first however, you must move the plot along from the presentation into the next step, using what we call, the false close.

## The False Close

The first step in Act Three is known as the False Close. You'll understand why it has that name in just a minute. This is the step you think you've been waiting for. You finally get to ask for the sale. Well are they going to buy or aren't they? An amateur will think they've made it when they get to this part. A novice might think, "Here it is, it's closing time. I've got this!"

So, let's ask for the sale. Easy, right? The first step is to recap with the prospect the benefits of what you're selling. This should be quick, one or two sentences. Here are some great routines you can use on this part of the false close: "So if I could show you a way to reduce [Pain Point #1], eliminate [Pain Point #2], and increase revenue…"
"If our services allow you to X, Y, Z…"
 "If my product allows you to increase THIS while reducing THAT…"

The second step is to then turn it into a question to which they can't, and wouldn't, say "no". For example, "Does that sound like something you would consider?"
"Would that be in line with your company's goals?"
"Would that be of interest to you?".

Of course the prospect will agree with that notion. Why wouldn't they? It's the truth. So they'll answer, "yes," obviously. Now, it might have been you that convinced them or you might have just gotten them to admit it where they wouldn't before. Either way, it's out in the open now. They've shown their cards. Their defense is down. You have their king in check. It's not yet a checkmate, though.

Watch what happens when you go in for the finishing move: Say something like, "Exactly! So listen, I can get you started right now. I'll prepare the paperwork for you, all I need is some basic information and your credit card details, fair enough?"

The prospect starts to squirm. Here comes the fun part.

**Overcoming Objections**

There comes a time in every sales conversation when the prospect begins to lose faith. Maybe they've been waiting politely for you to finish your spiel before they hit you with the old, "I'm not interested." or a quick, "we're happy with our current supplier." Maybe they want to buy but are afraid to admit it.

There are two main categories of objections. There are, of course, legitimate reasons someone might be unable or not wanting to buy, and then there are excuses. Legitimate reasons should have been discovered in the qualification phase. If you've gotten this far, the prospect can't say they don't have the money, because you know they do. They can't say they don't need the product or service, because you know they do. They can't say they need someone else to sign off on it, because you've already cleared with them that they are the decision-maker and have the authority. One legitimate reason that can be brought up at this point is, "I'm waiting for a loan to come through," or something along those lines. "I can't do it right now, but for sure later, on this specific date," is something you might encounter from someone who is excited about your opportunity but not quite ready to buy right then and there. Another could be that, maybe, they are really not impressed with the product or service you're selling. Then again, maybe they are just simply misunderstanding your offer. Regardless, legitimate reasons can be dealt with in real-world ways. If your prospect is waiting for approval on a loan and it's taking too long, perhaps help them look at other financing options. If they don't quite understand something about what you're selling, now's your opportunity to clear up any questions they might have. If your prospect does in fact like and want what you're selling but doesn't want to pay the top price, you might be able to direct them to a lower-cost economy option. Maybe you have the authority to offer a discount. If your prospect really does want the thing, they'll work with you to get around those obstacles and satisfy their needs.

Legitimate reasons are one thing, but then we have excuses. Excuse-type objections are defense mechanisms. When it comes time to put their name on the dotted line, the prospect, all of a sudden, panics and starts to think that if they buy from you and somehow end up regretting it, they'll feel, and look, stupid. Nobody wants to feel stupid. Everyone wants to be in the right and make the right decisions. Everyone wants to feel smart and be regarded by others as such. Excuse-type objections protect the prospect from what they think will make them look dumb. They don't want you to think they were an easy sell, or a pushover. Excuse objections are most often triggered subconsciously. The prospect will likely believe their excuse to be a legitimate reason; They aren't lying or making excuses in their own mind. For them, these excuses are a way to protect their integrity.

So don't get mad or frustrated when you hear a clear excuse. If you give up at the first sign of resistance and say, "well I guess it is what it is, nice talking to you," you'll never succeed. Never forget, you've gotten this far; this prospect is qualified. They have a need for what you're selling and they have the money for it. If you give up now you have wasted your time. Another salesperson will get your commission or the prospect will go to your competitor later when they come to their senses and decide they want to "shop around".

So how do you handle an excuse-type objection? First, sympathize with it - it is how they feel. Remember, in the moment, feelings are real. People will ignore facts when their feelings are stronger than their on-the-spot powers of analysis. People make decisions on a basis of pain versus pleasure. Cater to their feelings first. Start with something like, "I hear your concern," or "I totally get where you're coming from."

Next, ask another question that will force them to admit that they still like the idea and still have that need. Ask a question that boxes the prospect in and gets them to refute their own objection: "Let me ask you, does the idea of bringing in more revenue to your business make sense to you?"
"I have to ask, just to go back in our conversation a bit, you currently pay X for [Service] and only receive X, Y, Z benefits; Wouldn't you say you usually try to get the most for your money?"
"Would going through with a purchase today totally dry up your funds and put you in the poor house?"

Then get back to selling. Determine what the objection hints at below the surface. If you feel the objection stems from uncertainty about the product or service itself, go back over some features or benefits you did not list in your original presentation. Get them back into feeling that rollercoaster of emotions, and back at the conclusion that what you're selling will justly fill their void.

If you feel the objection stems from uncertainty or distrust of you personally, or of your company, you now have an obligation and opportunity to strengthen or rebuild rapport. Reestablish yourself to the prospect and reiterate your trustworthiness. Building rapport can be done very quickly, so long as you use language and tonality that says you really do care. Then, start to transition into how great your company is. Talk about how great of a place it is to work, and put a name and a face to the owner... Especially if you are the owner.

If the prospect is totally qualified but can't seem to find a real reason to hang up or walk away, even with all their excuses, hit them with a benefit of going ahead and buying right now. Maybe this is the last day of some sort of promotion, maybe enrollment will soon close for the year, maybe the company who's stock you are trying to sell the prospect is about to make an announcement of a new product and the price of a share will skyrocket. Urgency is key here.

If the prospect takes you through every excuse they can think of, has you refute and handle each one, yet stays uncertain and still refuses to end the conversation on their own, just flat out ask: "What's the real barrier that's preventing us from making a deal today?" Then work with the new objection or legitimate reason they give you as you would any other.

The worst objection is, "Let me think about it," because of how vague it is. With that statement, the prospect gives you nothing to work with. The fact is, if they were convinced and excited, they'd buy right now. The Hollywood Method was created to deal with almost any situation that could occur in a sale. So use it! Go through the objection handling process: Sympathize, ask a qualifying question to figure out the real trouble, get an agreement that they are still interested in reaping the benefits of the product or service and then get back to selling.

A subsequent chapter in this book will go through some of the most common objections and some routines you might use to overcome them. For now, though, a cursory overview of the process will suffice you in moving to the final stage where you can actually close the sale and make the transaction.

**True Close**

After the climactic battle of objections and excuses, it's time to make a deal. Once you feel the prospect's tone indicates trust and certainty, transition from the objections phase into the closing stage. This is basically a repeat of the False Close. Say something like, "Great, I'll prepare the paperwork right now, I just need your credit card information, fair enough?"

All legitimate and imagined arguments against buying have been neutralized. They say, "Fair enough!" and the exchange occurs. Congratulations! You've uncovered the secret formula. The secret formula to closing a sale is asking for it! So long as you've rightfully made it to this step, done everything right and haven't skipped anything, you should have no problem getting the final agreement here.

NOTE: After all that, after the whole performance, the prospect can still say, "no." Let me be clear: No means no. I'm not talking about excuses or objections, a real "NO" means you did something wrong. You didn't move them through the emotions you needed to move them through, you didn't give them a good enough logical justification, or maybe you were awkward and off-putting. Maybe something you said or did insulted the prospect. If you got past the qualification phase you know they are a perfect candidate. So, if after all is said and done, you've run them through all your excuse-busting routines, and they still give you a hard no: It was something you did in the last minute. I don't say this to discourage you, I say it to motivate you to practice and improve. Maybe you might check up on this prospect later in life. Who knows? A hard no can be replied to with only, "Okay, thank you for your time. Goodbye."

## Common Objections & How to Handle Them

When you've gone through this sales process many times over, you'll start to notice that prospects often come at you with identical objections. I'm not talking about the legitimate reasons someone might not be able or want to buy. I'm referring to those pesky excuse-type objections introduced in the previous chapter.

The objections you'll encounter are often the same because, as I mentioned, they are the prospect's defense mechanism when something is telling them that the pain of parting with their money outweighs the pleasure of whatever it is you are selling.

In the last chapter, I showed you the formula for dealing with excuse objections: First, acknowledge and sympathize with the objection. Then ask a qualifying question to figure out the real trouble. Next, get an agreement that the prospect is still interested in reaping the benefits of the product or service, and then finally, get back to selling. Sometimes, you can skip the qualifying question and go straight to the agreement. Sometimes you have to explain a bit more about your company or offering at this time as well. Use your judgment and adjust your approach according to trial and error.

These are the five most common objections you'll encounter in the field. They are not listed here in any particular order.

**First Objection:** "It's too expensive!"

**How to handle it:**

**Sympathize:** "I totally get that the money you spend is a concern for you."

**Ask a qualifying question:** "But I have to ask, just to go back in our conversation a bit, you currently pay X for [Service] and only receive X, Y, Z benefits; Wouldn't you say you usually try to get the most for your money?"

**Get an Agreement:** "So if your dollar is going further, wouldn't you say that's a good thing?"

**Second Objection:** "I need to talk it over with my team."

**How to handle it:**

**Sympathize:** "I hear your concern; your team's input is important to you, as it should be."

**Ask a qualifying question:** "But let me ask you, you are the leader of your team; ultimately, you make the executive decision, correct?"

**Get an agreement:** "So then as the leader, it's your responsibility to make the right choices for your company. When you make the right decisions and do right by your business, your team trusts and respects you even more, right?

**Third Objection:** "We only work with companies we know"

**How to handle it:**

**Sympathize:** "Oh I get that, there's a lot of choices out there and once you find a good one, you need to hold onto it."

**Get an agreement:** "Let me ask you though... If other companies in your industry/area trust us to handle this for them, and I can provide you some testimonials if you like, wouldn't you say it might be worth getting to know us a bit?" (They say, "sure, I guess.")

**Give more background on your company:** "Exactly! So we've been in business since [Year] and we've been helping businesses like yours accomplish blah blah blah blah…"

**Fourth Objection:** "That may work for other types of businesses but not mine."

**How to handle it:**

**Sympathize:** "I hear what you're saying. I totally understand it's important for you to make the right decisions for your very specific type of business, and you know your business best.

**Ask a qualifying question:** "I have to ask though, going back a bit, you said you have never done something like this, correct?"

**Get an agreement:** "So generally, you and I can both agree that if someone hasn't properly tried something they can't rightfully say it doesn't work, right?"

**Give more background on your company:** "Exactly, so we've worked with [Similar Company] for the last several years, and they can attest, we've been able to help them blah blah blah"

**Fifth Objection:** "I think I might want to shop around."

**How to handle it:**

**Sympathize:** "I get that; I agree, you should always be aware of the different options out there, especially with how many choices there are."

**Ask a qualifying question:** "But, I've got to say, what I'm offering you here has the best features and the highest quality in the market. Especially for the cost...so I have to ask you, does 'shopping around' mean you're just looking for the lowest price you can find?"

**Get an agreement:** "Well then, I don't know... if you're paying the absolute least amount possible for something, wouldn't you say you might, just maybe, be sacrificing quality?" (If you're feeling bold, you might tack on, "You're not the type of person who cuts corners are you?")

Once you understand the formula, you should be able to easily write your own routines and handle new and ever-evolving objections. When you are faced with an objection you haven't dealt with before, write it down and apply the formula. The next time it comes up, you'll be prepared to blast right through it!

# Ethics

Sales is not a one-sided affair. When you're with a prospect, you are simply two humans having an exchange. Ultimately, you might be able to help one another. Many salespeople don't get this concept. They see the prospect as a piece of raw meat that they can cook to extract that sweet, money juice flavor. In what world does that do any good? An unscrupulous telemarketer convincing an old senile woman to reverse mortgage her house, or a bogus minister selling "magic" water on late night TV does not do the world any good. The problem is, so many people worry so much about making a dollar that they neglect basic human decency. Don't neglect basic human decency. If not for the sheer goodness in your heart, at least for your reputation, which would surely suffer should people find out you operate insidiously.

A robust moral and ethical code is important to longevity in your sales career. The words, "morals" and "ethics" are often used interchangeably but they are different. While they both relate to "right" and "wrong," ethics refers to rules provided by an external source, like codes of conduct in workplaces or principles in religions. Morals refer to an individual's own personal values concerning what they believe to be right and wrong.

You might believe that morals are relative, and in part they are, but there are certainly universal moral concepts that anybody, in almost any era or society would attest to. So where do morals and ethics come from? The law? Well... It's obligatory that I tell you not to do anything illegal. It's obligatory that I tell you not to break the law. I can't tell you exactly what is legal or illegal in your area. I'm no lawyer. Laws vary from municipality to municipality, state to state, country to country. If you do something the government has declared to be illegal, they'll send men with guns to kidnap you. Laws are not necessarily based on morals or ethics. Each one was created with ulterior motives and written in legalese that the average person or politician can't even understand. Therefore, don't base your personal ethical system on what the law prescribes. Law is an implicit threat from a vicious, violent, mob.

Instead, you should develop your moral code on the basis of pain versus pleasure. It may be hard to believe when we look at the news or the events in the world around us, but most people will do anything to avoid causing another person pain. In sales, as in life, you should avoid causing pain to those who are innocent and undeserving. Your prospect is not an enemy. Your prospect is someone who needs your help, and on the flipside, your prospects are your livelihood. With this in mind, we start to uncover some universal morals.

The Golden Rule is the age-old moral principle that people should treat others how they would like to be treated. It encompasses all of the universal morals. The universal morals are the ethical system you should uphold, especially when using such powerful tools as the Hollywood Method to persuade others to bend to your will. In the words of the late, great, entertainment magnate, Stan Lee, "With great power, comes great responsibility." You must aim in your sales to maintain tolerance, consideration and compassion for the person you are dealing with.

Do not lie to your prospect by misrepresenting your offering or artificially inflating the price for the sole purpose of squeezing them. Do not attempt to back an unqualified prospect into a corner with objection handling routines and force them to buy something they don't need or can't afford. You should have no intention to do harm in any way, as the actions of a quality salesperson do more good than harm.

You should want to care about your customers' well-being so much that you continuously check up on them later to make sure they are still satisfied. It takes just one interaction to forge a life-long bond between a salesperson and customer. Don't sabotage a potential genuine connection by basing that first interaction (or any, for that matter) on untruths or strong-arm tactics.

Morals aren't something you have to go looking for in ancient texts or scriptures, either. Consider The Golden Rule when operating in life and in sales, and adopt it as your ethical system. Make it a facet of your inner game. By preserving a temperament of aiming to do no harm and doing unto others as you would have them do unto you, it is without a doubt that you will become the salesperson who everybody, and I mean everybody, prefers to deal with.

## Final Words

Ever since I created my first business, I have been selling every single day of my life. I've gone from being incredibly apprehensive about selling to looking forward to my next interaction. When I teach the system to others and watch their success, I'm overjoyed to see the method I developed in action, functioning in the real world, with real people.

I know what works and what doesn't work. The Hollywood Method is made up of the things that work. Plain and simple. Selling doesn't have to be an arduous task, or a chore. It can be a fun, exciting performance. A performance that nonetheless needs to be rehearsed and honed over many repeat recitals.

The people of the world need the products, services, and experiences you offer. They need you, the sales master, to help them achieve their goals, solve their problems, and fill their voids. You, the newly proficient salesperson uphold the honorable morals and ethics laid out in this book, and therefore, really are the person who should be out there doing this work. As you now know, there's a lot more to selling than just convincing someone to give you their money. Your job is to motivate people to make constructive moves in their lives.

Spread the good word. Help other people grow their business or advance their careers: Teach this system to others. Sell them this book! Just for practice...

## About The Author

Matt Lawrence is a serial entrepreneur and business developer. He holds the position of Chief Marketing Officer of New York City-based clothing brand Streetletic, as well as President and CEO of Long Island based inbound marketing firm, Choppa Media. He has made it his duty to help others pursue their dreams and make their living doing it. In addition to his numerous business ventures, he is an accomplished performer and recording artist with both label and independent credits to his name. He maintains two private music studios in Long Island, New York.

## Choppa Media

Choppa Media is Long Island's standout content creation firm. The premier provider of valuable and necessary creative solutions for businesses: Web and graphic design, photography and retouching, videography and video editing, audio production, social media marketing and consulting. Choppa Media's mission is to help businesses communicate more effectively, look better, sound better and reduce their advertising and marketing costs. Visit ChoppaMedia.com for more information, and don't forget to sign up for the mailing list to get exclusive priority access to special deals, as well as news about new and exciting books, products and services!

Printed in Great Britain
by Amazon